AF597946

The Melody of Love

Written and Illustrated by

JANINE RAINWATER

SOPHIA INSTITUTE PRESS
Manchester, New Hampshire

Cover design by Janine Rainwater with Emma Helstrom and Perceptions Studios.

Cover and interior artwork by Janine Rainwater.

Sophia Institute Press
Box 5284, Manchester, NH 03108
1-800-888-9344
www.SophiaInstitute.com

Sophia Institute Press® is a registered trademark of Sophia Institute.

hardcover ISBN 979-8-88911-402-4
ebook ISBN 979-8-88911-403-1

Library of Congress Control Number: 2024944134

First printing

To my mom, who has always inspired me to dream.

It was a lovely, peaceful night
Of glimmering moon and starshine bright.

On the fields grazed restless sheep
While cool wind over the plains did sweep.

A baby slept on cloth so soft
While a sea of stars twinkled aloft.

When down from Heaven's celestial light
A song was born, and Love took flight —

A glorious symphony whose sound …

… Awakened creatures all around.

The skies exclaimed! The earth resounded!

Across the fields stags leaped and bounded.

Moonlight gleamed through forest bright
As moose and bear danced in delight.

In depths of sea the song inspired
A playful, underwater choir.

The skies and seas and earth rejoiced
For Love had found its blissful voice . . .

. . . Within the tiny, sleeping Child,
So beautiful and meek and mild.

The message was a tale begun:
A Father's love for His own Son.

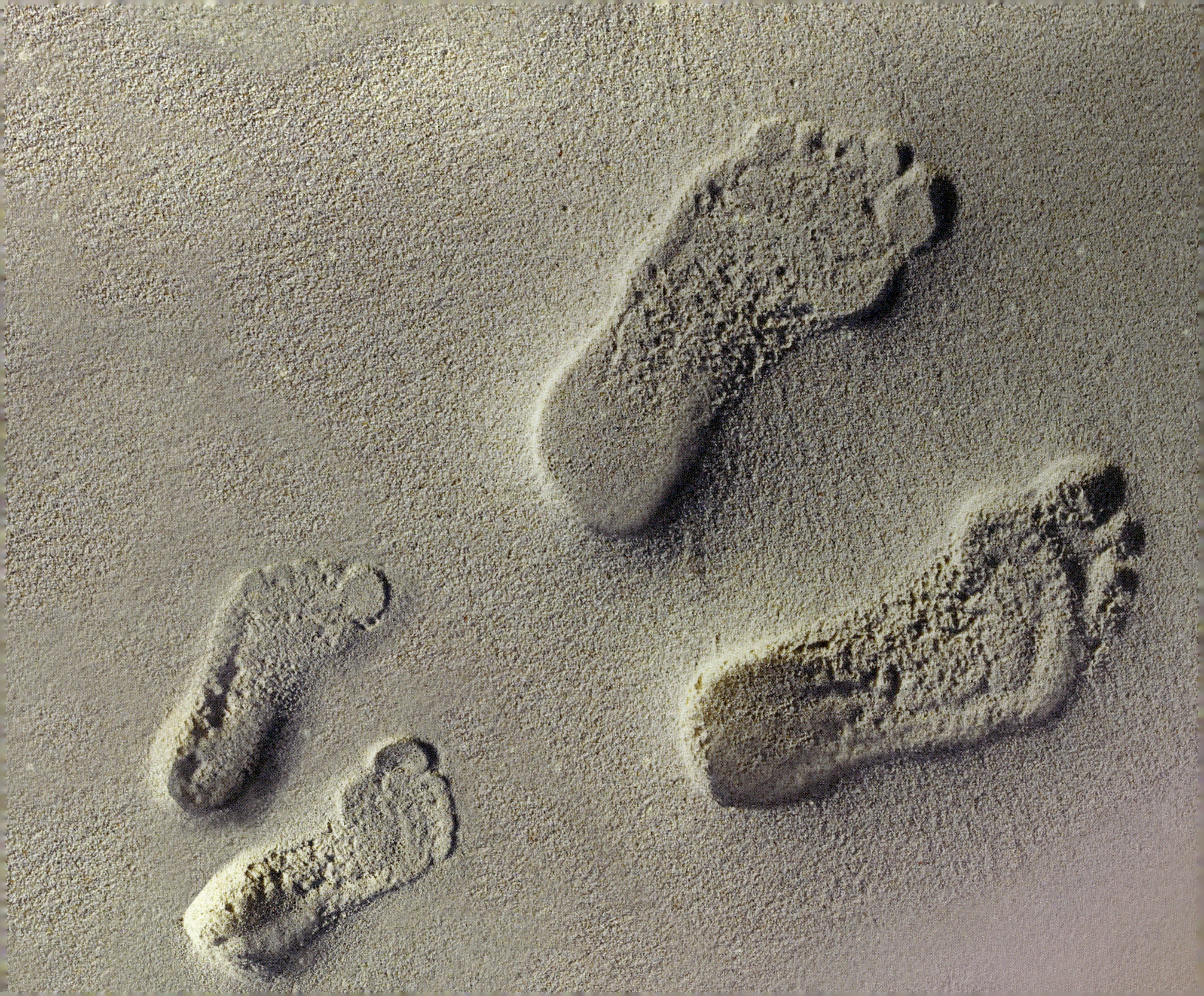

In time small hands and feet would grow,
And proof of boundless love would show.

But now His task was just to dream
While Love's refrain around Him streamed.

If you give heed, you still can hear
This melody of Love most clear.

So when that song
draws your heart near,
Know Love has found you;
You're loved, my dear.

About the Author and Illustrator

Janine Rainwater is an artist and graphic designer who is dedicated to creating heart-warming stories that capture the imaginations of young readers and their families. Janine is a lifelong follower of Jesus, and her faith deeply influences her work.

About

Sophia Institute

Sophia Institute is a nonprofit institution that seeks to nurture the spiritual, moral, and cultural life of souls and to spread the Gospel of Christ in conformity with the authentic teachings of the Roman Catholic Church.

Sophia Institute Press fulfills this mission by offering translations, reprints, and new publications that afford readers a rich source of the enduring wisdom of mankind.

Sophia Institute also operates the popular online resource CatholicExchange.com. Catholic Exchange provides world news from a Catholic perspective as well as daily devotionals and articles that will help readers to grow in holiness and live a life consistent with the teachings of the Church.

In 2013, Sophia Institute launched Sophia Institute for Teachers to renew and rebuild Catholic culture through service to Catholic education. With the goal of nurturing the spiritual, moral, and cultural life of souls, and an abiding respect for the role and work of teachers, we strive to provide materials and programs that are at once enlightening to the mind and ennobling to the heart; faithful and complete, as well as useful and practical.

Sophia Institute gratefully recognizes the Solidarity Association for preserving and encouraging the growth of our apostolate over the course of many years. Without their generous and timely support, this book would not be in your hands.

www.SophiaInstitute.com
www.CatholicExchange.com
www.SophiaTeachers.org

Sophia Institute Press® is a registered trademark of Sophia Institute.
Sophia Institute is a tax-exempt institution as defined by the Internal Revenue Code, Section 501(c)(3). Tax ID 22-2548708.